Helen Sheppard is a Bristol-ba
as a midwife. Her poetry exp
friendship, health and loss, a
unheard. She started to write
your reading' class. Helen co-r

GN00455324

Loves the alchemy of community events with Lyra Poetry Festival, PBH Free Fringe Candlelit sessions and performance of Voices of the Bedminster Coal Miners. She enjoys mentoring new poets. Helen has performed at Milk Poetry, Berkeley Square Review, Mind Matters, Persistant Sisters, That's What She Said, RTB Spotlight, Torriano Meeting House, Harvard Medical School and Nuyorican Poetry Cafe, schools parks and gardens. Helen's work has been published widely, including These are the Hands NHS Anthology, Commended in Hippocrates Prize 2017 Tools of the Trade - Poems for New Doctors, Under the Radar and Hecate Birth Anthology.

Helen is currently conducting interviews with extraordinary poets for her podcast *Health Beat Poets*, their 'take' on Poetry & Health

'Helen Sheppard writes about her own life as a mother, daughter and midwife, the poems are explicit and tender, a recasting of medical activity, reclaiming the appropriated pregnant female body in this relentless shamanic, muscular set of poems. Odes to her existential knowledge of midwifery, her powerful disobedient voice occupies the discarded feminine experience, in a fresh, humorous way. Silence contracts, sweats, births and deaths create the story of a whole women in this witty, self-possessed collection.'

Sarer Scotthorne

Fontanelle

To Vander,

So many stories...

Helen Sheppard

Helen Sheppard

Burning Eye

BurningEyeBooks
Never Knowingly
Mainstream

This edition published by Burning Eye Books 2021

www.burningeye.co.uk

@burningeyebooks

Burning Eye Books
15 West Hill, Portishead, BS20 6LG

ISBN 978-1-913958-10-7

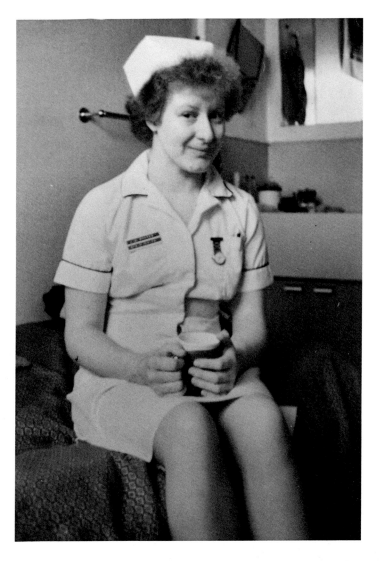

'FONTANELLE'
Burning Eye Books

Helen Sheppard

@HelenSheppard7
www.instagram.com/HelenSheppard58/
helensheppard58@gmail.com

Fontanelle

For Doreen

CONTENTS

Content Notice - This collection explores themes of a sensitive nature including: pregnancy, childbirth, mental health, child abuse, rape and medical stuff. This collection is all about the conversations, struggles and joys of caring for ourselves and others.

OPENING

A gestation reaches its timely conclusion.
Her muscled hammock softens, slackens.
I am with her wet slit, hands quiet, ready.

A head-down pressure, spine to belly.
Her womb now taut as a new balloon.
I hear heart beat code, pains come, go.

A tuft of hair appears, recedes to tease.
Her skin peels over a spongy first frown.
I map-read headland suture, fontanelle.

A flicker of eyelids, phantom of new.
Her hands clutch knees, chin tucks in;
I prop her heel on my hip, bear down.

A nose tips. Bloodline, too early to know.
Her guttural sounds, deep, old as Eve.
I breathe in rhythm between her pushes.

A fold of ear unfurls as lips pucker apart.
Her fingers reach over, stroke baby hair.
I loosen cord. A rough touch can mutilate.

A breath-held moment. Bruise-blue runs to red.
Her opening, forgotten, already starts to close.

SAFE HARBOUR

You're yet-to-become,
one cell collision.
You flex and stretch
and wallow in water,
all bump and tail.
You tether, then float,
wriggle to sea sounds.
Your heart drum-beats,
connects in shimmers.
Your wet dough brain.
You reach out to grasp,
tug your navel string.
Crouch down to engage,
then kick out to begin.

THERE IS NO ROOM 13 ON LABOUR SUITE

Room 14, I smile at a young woman clutching
a Care Bear. She says, *He rubbed up against
me.* She says, *I put a pill in my belly button.*

Her belly, inflated beneath baggy sweatshirt
and joggers. *Can you lie back? Let's make you
comfortable. Yes, of course your bear can stay.*

*My tummy hurts, make it stop, I'm going to die.
Is anyone with you today?* She shakes her head.
I'll have a look at your tummy, then we can talk.

My rubbed hands rest on a plateau, measure,
trace sides, fingertips walk a ridge of spine.
Breath deep – I feel a head nested in her pelvis

I draw her, draw baby within, name them.
We stroll quiet corridors, the city lit below,
caught up in rhythums of surge and spasm
labour lost in a movie of her own making.

She lays her bear in the crib, crouches,
retches into transition, whimpers, sways
primal with purpose, on all fours, pushes.

She births quickly, sits back, scoops newborn
into her arms – *It's a baby.* – *Yes, your baby.*
Quietly, we count ten fingers and ten toes.

ONE WAY TO BIRTH A PLACENTA

Wait…

New mum and baby

      rest in bed

        at home

in candle light

      incense cones

        rainforest sounds

Wait…

      Women friends

        raspberry leaf tea

          soft chants

Wait…

Mum cuddles

      baby to breast

        latches to suckle

Wait…

Mum closes eyes

      baby murmurs

        first sounds

Wait...

Woman swaddles baby

       mum sips tea

                   cord   lengthens

Wait...

Small gush of blood

       separation

          drops in bucket

Wait...

Cord stops pulsing

       cut and tie

          blood loss in a jug

Wait...

Check afterbirth

       smooth edge

          two-layer membrane

Wait...

Fry with onions

or

       plant under rose bush

WITH WOMAN

Nurses and midwives were once treated as witches,
charms and incantations used to ward off demons in labour.
Midwifery was legally recognised profession in 1902.

VIRGINS

We emerge as virgins from our mothers' wombs.
Celia is chosen to play Mary in the school nativity.
I cut threads of her golden, shoulder-long hair,
wear a shepherd's towel over my not-right crew cut.

LIFE'S POND

NICU: Neonatal Intensive Care Unit.

Breath of feathers.
Two-finger press-ups to chest.
Monitor beeps back.

Doctors capsule chat
behind closed doors; parents smell
coffee roasting.

Expert hands, soft touch.
'Life's pond' inside clingfilm skin.
A breath-held moment.

DOREEN PACKS PETTICOATS MADE OF PARACHUTES

Inspired by my aunt Doreen, born 1922.

Nurse/Midwife 1941–1976.
Midwifery care £3, forces' wives £2/6.
NHS 1948 – free.

She practises injections of penicillin,
loaded a silver bullet for syphilis.

Prays for uncomplicated births, hears
of prem babies left by open windows.

She does visits on a rickety pedal cycle
in winters of power cuts, too cold for terry

nappies to dry. Trudges through snowdrifts,
wears a hot water bottle tied under layers.

She treats: hungry beaten children, pox
in London smog, constantly combs nits.

One day off duty a month. Watches royal
Elizabeth's wedding with scone and knitting.

She dresses Miss Muzzle's legs, covered in
coal dust and ulcers. Mrs Spencer makes

custard with her breast milk to satisfy
husband's desires, spoons cow's milk

into her baby. The other nine children
play out somewhere till it's tea time.

Her worst day, a young mother bleeds
to death and a filthy house in Willesden.

A great day, meeting Kevin, whom she
delivered sixty years ago, with all his family.

HELEN PACKS CASSETTES AND BLACK STOCKINGS

Nurse/Midwife 1976–2000.
Midwifery care free: NHS.
Natural childbirth and informed choice 1970s.

She is curious about how twins are born,
hopes not to lose anyone she delivers.

She fills a birthing pool while birth
partner strips off. Whale music plays,

no need for a fishing net. Mother births,
baby swims, family breathe gently as one.

One day she undresses a baby for a weigh.
Finds a cigarette burn on a week-old thigh.

HIV arrives in maternity. Mask, gown, glove
up. Try to be kinder and wait for some cure.

Doctor says if your hand touches infected
blood, it's safe to wash with soapy water.

Today Princess Di is buried. A group of men
kick her car for working with no respect.

She dodges riots, weighs babies in crack
houses, and drinks chai with a family who

give her a frilly pink polyester dress for her
daughter, and a box of rose sweetmeats.

Her worst day, home visit to a newborn,
blue, breathless, and parents say all is well.

A great day, having poem on first delivery
published, celebrating birth with Doreen.

MAGPIES, 1880

An aproned service girl kneads
dough at dawn, scours dirty pans
with sand. My great-grandmother.

Great-grandfather cracks his shackles,
a free man, merchant seaman,
migrates Atlantic in filth and salt

to London docks, coal-black. Enchanted
in shadows of an East End tavern,
a mixed opalescent pair, eyes bright

by gas light. Her belly swells, births,
leaves charcoal foundling on a doorstep.
My grandfather soothes his mother's

last suckle. Wakes to thread shiny
charms to aunt's apron ties. Some say
this child is Brazilian, or from less

riotous parts of America. Never Africa,
always too incendiary. Family secrets
scatter, as magpies fly away to roost.

MOTHERSHIP

Un-be-come   one cell   blue-print   Be-coming
multiple   millions
contained   confined
cord pulses in shadow water
tethers my mothership to me
her salt tears of joy and fear spill
they seep into this body and bone
drain into a fragile equilibrium
our hearts race to a faster
Beat   Beat   Beat
feet walk walls
kick snow on
mountain
peaks
head
down
ready to
wear her
pelvic
crown

New

FISH FINGERS AND BAKED BEANS

I remember door knocks, neighbours:
in labour, borrowing tenners for gas,
private Clearblue pregnancy tests.

I remember delivering a dead baby,
being cathartically sick on merlot,
waking on Anna's sofa under blankets.

I remember forgetting to collect my kids
from school, delayed by an emergency
C-section. Tina dished out snacks and telly.

I remember picnics in snow and torrents,
tree climbing, mudslides. Picking up
our shredded threads of mothering.

I remember, one night, the kids taking
turns projectile vomiting off bunk beds
and a long list of home visits next day.

I remember waste, strikes, cuts in care,
mountains of recording, litigation dread,
fish fingers and baked beans for a week.

I remember sobbing in your kitchen,
resignation letter sealed and stamped.
I remember to toast many mothers.

HOW TO FINGER-PAINT FONTANELLES

How to map-read headland sutures and soft spots.
Foetal skull muscle thrusts through birth canal.
Pelvic bones displace, make space in labour.
I insert index/middle finger to feel vaginal braille.
Trace trajectory of passage, power and passenger.
Mind will adjust to this darkness, seek landmarks.
Still fingers, foetus curls with contractions, rotates.
Reach to feel skull plates shift in membranes.
Fingertips sketch overlaps, ridges moulding to fit.
Assess engagement, suboccipito-frontal diameter.
I feel vaginal wall stretch to capacity, fully dilated.
Explorers, cartographers: mother, foetus and midwife.
Open my eyes, smile, slowly withdraw my fingers.
Mum and baby together tuck chins into chest.
Each push a new landscape, foetal head, fontanelle.
I fold away my birthing maps for next delivery.

DOREEN BALANCES ON A PLINTH

Doreen skips school,
snips chrysanthemums
with her trench-head dad.

In service and drudgery
she scrunches the Daily
Herald to set parlour fires.

Evacuees arrive. Her task:
to scrub city boys clean
of swagger and desires.

They give lip and fancy
words. Doreen learns her
letters, applies to nurse.

She swaps food rations
for sturdy brown brogues
from a rogue at the door.

Dodges doodlebugs to
dress wounds and deliver
babies in sooty terraces.

She knows poultices
soothe, and treats bomb
wounds with kindness.

Doreen says she's lived
life aplenty for a thick
kid from the village.

ODE TO OUR MATERNAL BONES

our mother carries us big and high
doctor says to expect a strong boy

our mother's blood pressure sky-flies
she births us, twins, undiscovered

our mother tries to feed her sparrow
babies, constant squawks to snatch

our mother's nipples, raw and bloody
we squabble for a pecking order

our mother takes prem twins home
while dad starts an evening class

our mother on a whim demands
the vicar save us from evil ways

our mother's womb is cut away
she brings home fish and chips

JOY OF MY MOTHER'S PINK LEAFLET

My mother dishes up spag bol on a too-hot day in '72.
She forgets to buy tomatoes and nowhere sells basil.

My mother says, *We need to shop for underwear.*
She stares at my yellow T-shirt and growing buds.

My mother says, *Have you read* that *pink leaflet?*
She says, *No need for questions; it's self-explanatory.*

My mother's leaflet has line diagrams and no glossary.
She's wedged it between *Forever Amber* and *Poor Cow.*

My mother's busy; I have torch and Radio Luxembourg.
She later pulls at my polo neck, a bruise, slaps my legs.

My mother retrieves *Valley of the Dolls* from my room.
She doesn't know I've hidden Dad's book, *Joy of Sex.*

VIRGINS

Mum says, *Keep it private till it's permanent.*
A neighbour, Stan, wakes me, jabs my flower.
Mum says, *Men drink and do that sort of thing.*
When I'm ready, I'll bring fireworks and gateau.

STITCHES

She watches her gramps pluck partridge, pull gizzards, heart.
Later, snatches partridge and stitches together with button
thread, darning needle, then gets feathers from the yard.
She tucks partridge into nan's hairnet, weaves in feathers,
then lobs her new pet into the sky. It wedges in a pear tree.
A doctor wears bauble earrings, tinsel-wrapped stethoscope.
In the operating theatre she replaces her gramps's heart.
Her stitches, now practised and neat, come together to seal.

ENDORPHINS

birth and sex
are the same
same hormones
same sensations
same anatomy
same brain
same vulva
same clitoris
same kissing
same masturbation
same relief

SELF PORTRAIT ON BIRTH

Part 1
I'm a midwife mother-to-be
bring labouring essentials
glucose tablets
cold compress flannel
pure oil of lavender
arnica to heal
I forget studying Myles Midwifery
statistically I won't die
I hope to be no trouble
I may grunt/scream/swear/hit/sue
I forget to book a birthing pool
or bring a personal playlist
natural pain relief if possible
please
avoid forceps – ventouse – C-section
try to leave me intact
I need everyone here – nobody near
I lose myself
I gain myself
I'm handed a baby
at home I cry watching Live Aid
wait for its mother
remember it's me

Part 2
I dance with a bawling toddler
to the Pogues' 'Sally MacLennane'
back to groin cramp waves
a month too early
I remember this grubby stuff
I forget giving birth
I hear nothing
as scrap bundle is whisked away

my belly feels full of kicks
I wash
sit on a bed
in a ward full of new births and babies
I have a phone number to call
mine warms up in a goldfish tank
in a place I've worked nights
I don't call
I wait
till our eyes meet
skin to skin

Part 3
at home
midwife, colleague, friend
I lean over the bannister
broken boiler
puddle bath of lukewarm water
in the front room
Freddie Mercury tribute concert plays on the telly
through the bands I sway
flop over the sofa
as head crowns I remember
I don't like this bit
Bowie and Lennox sing 'Under Pressure'
I scoop baby
we watch the concert
feast on mugs of tea
and cheese pickle sandwiches
in the morning our bed writhes
child-toddler-newborn

MY MOTHER IS PUT ON THE LIVERPOOL CARE PLAN

choice   withdraw   invasive   care

feeding   no-resuscitation   palliative   dying

hospice   hospital   home   hostel

everyone   expected   to   die

hastens   over-prescription   pain   relief

without   consent   drink   eat

condition   prognosis   respect   wishes

need   sensitive   communication   decisions

plan   treatment   information   symptom

control   fear   release   individual

review   neglect   cruel   conversation

fight   breath   fades   wait

                                        withdraw

The Liverpool Care Plan was developed in the late 1990s to provide best possible care for dying patients. Abolished in 2013 following a government-commissioned review which heard hospital staff wrongly interpreted its guidance, leading to stories of patients who were drugged and deprived of fluids in their last weeks of life.

'NO FLOWERS, PLEASE'

In hospital, when my mother breathes
her last, nurses remove a mug of teeth
while I eat bacon butties at her bedside,

then stroke a stray hair with my licked
fingers. Tip five drops of pure lavender
oil on a – *no flowers, please* – plastic plant.

STUDENT NURSE – ONE MONTH IN

Dear Mum and Dad,

I've learnt 'what's a nurse?' and how to admit patients,
about nits, how to make beds with envelope corners.

I clean a woman's wounds; she rarely eats or bathes,
sleeps at night on park benches under the Times.

I wash a man with an artificial leg. He makes a rag
rug from spare trouser legs for battle-axe matron.

I'm ordered to give him an inhalation. Later sister
pulls around curtains; he looks peaceful, dead.

DEEP PEARLS

teen on my doorstep
holds out her forearm

wrapped in tea towels
held by clingfilm

we sip instant coffee
while I unroll layers

her deep cut unfurls
into strings of pearls

MELANCHOLIA

I shadow Liz, who observes Alex,
with artery cuts and chemical tricks
his body concocts. They chat, share

smokes, shag behind haematology.
I later hear they've moved away,
have kids, are good for each other.

It's ECT Tuesday; Archie, a lawyer,
worries aliens will poison his meds.
He dresses in fine threads, trilby

and monocle. We set up chess;
he wins, unzips his fly, Joker's-grin
jerks off. I'm a little girl again.

June was caught out of wedlock
and baby taken. Over sixty years
a straitjacket hugs her hollow.

I wash daubs of shit off grey walls,
she soothes pillow creases tenderly,
her false teeth jiggle as she smiles.

Sore heads of mad mothers, soldiers,
puzzle solvers, firestarters. I sneak
drug trolley sleepers to ease bruises

from nursing in this nest of birds.
While McMurphy weeps, I crash
and burn; it's contagious. Let's talk.

JUNE

June wears a pillbox hat securely pinned,
a wedding band lent by a knowing friend.

June lies on newsprint, skirt hitched to her waist,
knees apart, gin-dozy, a new life scraped away

June feels unlucky. Out of wedlock, her belly
grows rounder in service for landed gentry

June hides under arches, charges three pence
a time. Arrested by bobbies, forbidden to speak.

June's thrown into an asylum as a pauper nurse,
eats mash and gravy daily, starts feeling kicks.

June has pains, is given a drum of caustic rum,
her 'fallen' baby taken, filling breasts bound.

June dabs sedative sores with beaten egg white,
forgets: birds, music hall songs, her little one.

HAIR

Growing up in small towns,
hairdressers offer crew cuts,
curlers, wigs in severe bobs.
In cities my fuzz is flat-ironed,
acid-straight, topiary-trimmed.

In cosy bars, strangers clink
pints on our table. Sweep
sweaty palms across tips
of my frizzy topknot.
If every hair molester paid

for fondles, I'd be on easy
street. Their fingers skim
my follicle ends on buses,
at gigs, in queues for the loo
in blatant barnet abuse.

After Saturday flicks Mum
cuts gum nests out my afro.
I withdraw pencil javelins
thrown onto our scattered
family of chess pieces.

VIRGINS

At a local school, three girls run, become brides,
while others have their womanhoods slashed.
Seventy-two virgins, promised as heavenly passports,
and gender rights and #MeToo finally fought.

MUNDANE SUNDAY, 1997

My babysitter's mother phones
while the sun shines,
when semi-skimmed runs out
and toast burns again.
Mandy's gone.
Gone where?
I swing my baby in a park as
Mandy's blood flows
down steps in our street,
twenty-seven stabs.
'Born Slippy' plays at her funeral.
Her long legs danced
through the nineties.
Sassy words share
Clearblue scares.
Nobody speaks.

PUNK

us straight-edge punks
start the party, then knit

hide genders in PVC rips
vegan DMs, snot-green

liberty spikes. we snort
sherbet, not aircraft glue

and catch Donita Sparks'
tossed tampon to compost

clear dance floors of glass
and safety pin emergencies

our sounds: Minor Threats
of metal down chalkboard

ballpoint tattoos count
in this poets' revolution

we keep our pants tight
as giving birth ain't punk

MY MOTHER'S STATIONERY CASE

Dear Mum,

I scatter your ashes.
Open your red leather stationery wallet. Its zip works perfectly.
In a plastic pocket are three black-and-white passport photos.

One, you with short black hair determined to curl to a softer style,
eyebrows drawn impeccably, lips painted Estée Lauder cranberry.
Your smile I don't recognise. This photo is ripped along an edge

where you unattached Dad one time. On your wide seventies collar
a Wedgwood brooch, a couple walking under a tree canopy, I
bought for your birthday with savings from boring Saturday jobs.

There's another split double photo taken in a Woolworths booth.
I remember my twin cut away her half when I left home,
our first day as separates. I have Dad's half-smile framed by spots.

In a stamp slot is your Pitman Shorthand 'mini' list of short
forms and contractions. Shorthand classes took you to hospitals,
note-taking for heart surgeons during the first British transplants.

A newspaper notice: *The bride, attired in a dress of white tulle
over taffeta embroidered with pearls and diamanté.* You paid
for your dress and flowers. *Her bouquet: cream roses, stephanotis,*

lily of the valley. Waxy blooms, exotic fragrances. You and Dad,
in a press release, embrace beside a three-tier wedding cake.
Before my wedding day, you give me money to buy a single bed.

A news story falls onto the floor. A photo of you grinning, holding
a food processor you won in a weekly crossword competition.
Tucked at the very back of your red leather stationery wallet

is a note I wrote after my first month training to nurse.
You gave me a pack of notelets, asked me to share every detail.
This one has a girl in a sombrero, writing, in a field of tulips.

ESCAPADES WITH DAD

Dad says when we are first born
our stomachs are the size of walnuts.
He spews up his gut full of fears, tiny
cannibals who eat and eat and…
shares his cheese pickle sandwiches.

Dad teaches me to slide a rule.
He says logarithms and amoebae
are proof of our existence, computers
will devour our facts and, remember,
pies are always square, never round.

Dad lies belly-down over cliffs
at Land's End. Tells me to straddle
his ankles. He reaches for rocks
for his rockery. We body-pivot,
stretch. Rocks splurge into squall.

Dad sleeps behind door locks.
Hospital ghosts float too close.
He puckers to kiss and spit pills.
Pockets full of drop-stitch holes
trail crumbs from chair to bed.

SILENT CHESS

Dad teaches me to play silent chess
as we suck splinters of treacle toffee.
Sometimes he vanishes from home.
Bored, I count his line of pill bottles.

As we suck splinters of treacle toffee,
family quirks once seemed ordinary.
Bored, I count his line of pill bottles,
unworthy of any mental connection.

Family quirks once seemed ordinary,
then I burn out and stare at a road kill.
Unworthy of any mental connection,
I fade and forget to feed my children,

then I burn out and stare at a road kill.
Sometimes he vanishes from home.
I fade and forget to feed my children.
Dad teaches me to play silent chess.

BLUE

One wintry Saturday afternoon, I tip my nan's
sewing box out. She isn't dead, just overseeing what's
long inside. Each cantilevered compartment a rainbow
of embroidery threads, poppers in pairings, knicker
elastic, mushroom darner, skirt and bra extenders

for when women quietly bloat. Hundreds of fruit drop
buttons stored separately in a shortbread biscuit
tin. I make a brew, we read news stories on back
of handmade patterns. In an envelope are years-old
newssheet shapes for a baby's bonnet never stitched.

I read a headline, *Infant dies as father performs
operation at home*. I cut two slices of fruit cake, wait.
'Poor boy, collapsed, bronchitis. His father Dr
Smith, lovely man, intelligent talker, cut open son's
chest with a razor blade. The mother left soon after.'

Nan picks out blue ribbon, 'He always was a dear
lad,' winds around a bobbin, secures with a pin.

CHILD AND I

A sparrow boy arrives at my door.
He drops empty into this flatpack city,
sleeps tonight where no bullets fly.

Dreams.

It's dark.

Water ice.

Black fins of shark.

Our languages are mismatched.
At breakfast I cook scrambled eggs.
He pinches clouds of sourdough.

As petals, they float in his bowl of warm milk.

WHEN LADY DI'S FUNERAL IS JUST ANOTHER DAY TO CARE

when you shrug on a navy midwife gabardine

when you hope for an uneventful Sunday shift

when you accept a cuppa at third home visit

when newborn baby Shane gains weight

when you carry bag and scales back to car

when two men approach, kick your bumper

when they wrench off both your wing mirrors

when they shout you've no respect for Lady Di

when you start ignition and drive away shaking

when a grandmother next visit gives sweet chai

when mum and baby snuggle in layers of sari

when a house of working girls are happy to chat

when you visit crack houses for antenatal checks

when a corner is cleared for midwife and bag

BURNOUT

Dear Mum,

When we meet I perch on a sofa at the far end / knees tucked up tight / feet hover off the carpet / face scrunches in twisted tissues / we wait as long as it takes / I have run out of life / burnt-out, my words flow as a temperamental tap / I write 2003 on a document, when the year is 2020 / I agree to our sessions / next session I say I plan to sit with plants / I talk about zombie dreams / I say 'they' judged from the day I was born / all 5 lb, plum-coloured, limp and little / my work email inbox is over 323 a week – unread / no reply comes to mind / I say I juggle watermelons and food tastes of soggy cardboard / I mention a painting at work made me sick / I blurt out my doctor has written me off / with work-related stress / as I leave today's session, I mention a steel bar wedged in my throat / we stand still while I flick-kick tingles away / I phone to say I can't come today / I have many appointments: occupational health – a teacher to see – an empty fridge / I come / slide a little nearer / my feet reach the carpet / I point to a vase of my favourite flowers / I say my brain is less full of bees / I look for circles and square edges on pictures and plant pots / today I bring printed words of when I hurt / glue on a roll of lining paper / stick a timeline of trauma / unroll lots of blank paper / sit quietly / I say when I was three Dad collapsed on the floor / I watched ambulance men / Dad disappeared / for Christmas that year – I unwrapped a nurse's uniform / pill pot / stethoscope / fob watch / bandages / thermometer / from that day caring was my life / I sit straight / talk slower / soles of my shoes reach the ground / I leave behind poems…

CINEMATIC SEIZURE

I shelter in an arthouse cinema
shelter from summer storms

storms in my head
storms kept hidden
hidden in a zoom
hidden to escape
escape room
escape afternoon
afternoon flicks
afternoon fits
fits shiver neurologist
fits blink
blink bark
blink spark
spark brain
spark dreams
dream speak
dream dirty
dirty devil
dirty fever
fever crowds
fever feature
feature silence
feature screams
scream pits
scream screen
screen seats
screen pop
pop boom
pop corny
corny creatures
corny music
music scratches
music sound shift
shift synaesthesia

shift senses
sense sonnets
sense soothsayer
soothsayer shouts
soothsayer claps
claps a rhythm
claps clicks kicks
kicks chair backs
kicks a beat
beat a cause
beat a kudos

I shelter in a cinema
shelter from storms

JULIE ANDREWS

Police are called to a disturbance. They find
me in an alley behind a theatre. I believe
I'm astride my lover, hands at their throat.

Every Tuesday since, I visit this room.
It shifts shape; sometimes a painting melts
from musicians into parrots in full flight.

Angle-poise light casts a soft glow over
one thing that never changes: my shrink.
They have my mother's smile, and point
to the only empty chair. I feel the paunch
of my belly swell black fabric of my habit.

As I talk the room chills into an igloo for one.
My skin hangs in folds, joints of my shoulders
dislocate. I slide off chair, coil into my womb.

Wake to see my shrink's salmon-pink shift dress
switch to a ballgown with huge cerise peonies.
I carefully spread the black skirt hem around me.

Can you see amazing colours?
                              Have I told you my name?

BIRTH WITH OR WITHOUT BOMBS

i
Twenty-four weeks, she spots, bed rest, watches TV.
9/11 plays out on repeat. Cortisol rises.
She was careful not to lift anything heavy.

ii
Home to toxic dust, ready for tigers.
Buoyant by birthing in a warm pool.
Dead faces press against windows.

iii
Bears down, breathes, calls her man.
They birth, hide under another blast.
No one notices space on the Polaroid.

iv
Home birth cancelled, keeps them safe.
She coughs into mask, newborn bathed.
Baby suckles, mother's smile concealed.

TAKE A SEAT IF…

your skin is pierced by bullets
smothered in tar and feathers

if policies censor your tongue
or they cut you for acceptance

if injustice stones your words
and tapes a twisted meaning

if you are coerced by bullies
or cyber screens exploit you

your rights are stripped away
innocently caught in air strikes

or crawl across hostile borders
if your scrap of land is torched

work drops you to your knees
and drug running isn't a choice

if your mind wobbles with terror
or spirits held dear are denied

bombs strapped on in honour
if they sentence tender kisses

PORCELAIN

in my workplace stairwell
hangs a self-portrait
by a young woman
of a waif of a girl
who squats, losing blood

each time I pass by
a memory colours in

this waif of a girl
waits for a boy
almost a man with easy smile
he makes her laugh
fourteen and new to love

he tells her to fly
they go for a drive
she tries a toke
he says breathe
hold smoke in your throat

he gives her a phone
all contacts his own
she answers, night, day
men waiting to rape
this unready girl

one day, warm breath on lips
her rape angel grows

feather down wings pierce
unfurl, she takes flight
this grace of a girl
scream
shatters her porcelain face

VIRGINS

Virgins, anti-heroes, comedy objects of ridicule,
horror, farce. They bleed to keep demons at bay,
to feed vampires mortality. Is virginity invented
as a gift to cherish or steal from anyone, at any age?

A PERSONALISED GUIDE FOR PEOPLE WHO ARE TRAVELLING TO ROTTERDAM AND STILL HAVEN'T QUITE DECIDED HOW THEY FEEL ABOUT PEOPLE

Collaborative poem with poet Callum Wensley for Lyra Poetry Festival.

> 1)   Your dark sense of humour might get a giggle from your close friends, but the people you're sharing a dorm with haven't learnt yet that you're not the dangerous kind of 'weirdo with a beardo'.

Check-in – New York, lifetime trip.
Yes, I packed my bag myself.
You're one kilogram over; repack or fine.
I repack, hand over my passport
and visa. They're mismatched;
you cannot fly. I plead and cry…
Sliding doors, time shifts.

> 2)   Have you developed the necessary interpersonal skills to engage in conversation? If someone hears your accent and assumes that your shared nationality is enough reason to start up a dialogue, try not to open with, 'If we were in Bristol right now, would we be having this conversation?' because the obvious answer is no, and they might then ask you why you are the way you are.

I find a quiet spot under a tree in
Rotterdam to flop; it's not exotic.
I read poetry to still my paranoia
when a woman says, Sitting on
grass at your age concerns us.
I close my book, walk away.
Sliding doors, time shifts.

I trudge through marshland, wade
in waters where bustling villages
and hushed windmills once stood.
Now it's a twenty-first-century shopper's
mecca. A giant metal horseshoe,
all steel, sheets, cables and glass.
Sliding doors, time shifts.

In a food hall with horns of plenty
jabbering tourists go Dutch, buy
syrup discs of… stroopwafel,
salt pickled herring and bottles
of pale ale. I've enough euros for
a bag of dragon's breath sweets.
Sliding doors, time shifts.

A boar head on a sausage stall
speaks, asks if I'm feeling okay
today, suggests I keep my head
down. Next moment it rains fish
and neon dragonflies divebomb,

the market becomes frenzied.
Sliding doors, time shifts.

> 6) No, really. Don't smoke pot.

A bloke stares at me slantways;
he checks his phone; if he moves
any nearer I'll stab him with my pen
and shout, *I'm no terrorist, I'm an
unofficial alien.* Then I recognise
that beard, those kind twinkle eyes…
Sliding doors, time shifts.

> 7) Okay, so you're going to ignore steps five and
> six. Okay. Well, then make sure your poker face is on
> point, because you might stumble upon a person you
> have a great amount of respect for. You may then
> have to spend the next forty-five minutes talking like
> you're not off your face, all the while thinking:
>
> *Oh, fuck. Helen Sheppard is here and she knows I'm
> high and I genuinely could be the first person to die
> from embarrassment!*

Sliding doors, time shifts.

BUBBLES

It takes time to feel comfortable in a war zone.
At 8pm your family clap, holler hope, give thanks.

A five-minute break, slurp of coffee, half a doughnut.
My hands crack from their thousand-a-day scrubs.
Your ventilation soundtrack: breath shunts and beeps.
I cool you, drain you, cleanse you, oxygenate your lungs
with their lesions from beautiful microscopic aliens.
A tornado of experts keep you here, flatten this curve.
I'm raw with sores behind my ears from mask elastic cuts.
Stitch groups make headbands with big buttons
and builders send PPE – their protection in demolition.
I'm practised, not hardy, cry briefly as beds fall empty.
Staff share an inappropriate joke and my smile is back.
In the next bed, a sister (mild asthma), a dad (angina),
a mum (diabetic), a son (misses playing football).
I find a tube in my coat pocket, given instead of confetti
at a wedding, blow bubbles at the end of tough shifts.
We meet in this pandemic together, intimate strangers.

Tonight we stay back, share donated prosecco, order
takeaways paid for in kind. Tomorrow I will sleep.

WISDOM IN LOCKDOWN

our memories fill bookshelves
read us in sepia or dazzling

see us as inspired, not infirm
when we swap feet for wheels

say our hair looks gorgeous
if it's straight as pump water

we've witnessed great changes
and each day is out of the blue

our adventures are for sharing
especially when our eyes close

BIRTH FOR EVERY BODY, 2050

For your midwife is part angel, cyborg, ordinary.
For your organs will not define your roles in birth.
For they know everyone will attract viruses and love.
For a womb, choose: self-made, donated, knitted within.
For midwives know persona labels and marmalade are extinct
For virtual visits, imagine warm hands, data scrutiny, telepathy.
For desirable traits and cherubs, click online foetal farms.
For bearing, be bold, write a wishlist for life and breath and sleep.
For feeding progeny, choose: human, plant or creature milk.
For advice on tears, bed sharing and co-parenting – take a quiz.
For early, adopted or surrogate baby, top up with wonderment.
For times you can't 'stop' sadness, dazzle days will come.
For your birth will not be sanitised.
For you are part: earth, blessed Gaia, and ordinary.

ALONE IN THE STORM

Our favourite walk. *Park up by the church*,
says the note under a jar of local honey.
It's March. I walk as Storm Ciara thrashes,
a hail hoolie with wind speeds over forty.
A spit of land splits the estuary – layer cake
of pea-green weed, grey waves, dashing
stratus clouds. I trudge muddy rock pools
among banks of acid-yellow gorse, coarse
grasses. Catkin caterpillars wriggle in the wind.
One surfer skims in slalom on a red board.
Seagulls leave snail trails of empty shells,
appetisers before they filch fish suppers.
Squally showers fall, life scours to bare
breath, then comes a fleeting quickening.

THINGS I NOW KNOW

Warm hands: first step to care.
Nurse, with a vivid imagination.
Illness demands community.
Caring is fifty percent intuition.

NHS have no magic wands.
Time is still; we fly through.
A prescription is not a cure.
There is no known sleep bank.

Disgust protects us from disease.
Snorkelling is a suckling reflex.
Mothers feed any open mouths.
Love tears us apart and binds us.

ACKNOWLEDGEMENTS

Thank you for listening to my poetry, reading it and sharing it with family and friends. It means a lot.

A huge thank-you to Bridget and Clive at Burning Eye Books for following my poetry journey and recognising when I was ready for this collection.

I came to poetry through burnout, and a 'kickstart your reading' class at Bristol Folkhouse, where I wrote my first poem in my forties. Then I tagged along to poetry open nights; thanks for your warm welcome, Andi Langford-Woods. They are my essential resource to hear a wide range of poets, try out new material and connect with other artists. Thanks to online and live readings, performances, workshops and writing groups, they developed my writing from shy scribblings to writing a collection.

There isn't room to thank all the generous, exceptional poets within the Bristol and wider poetry communities. Thanks to friends and writing buddies Pauline Seawards, Sarer Scotthorne, Lucy English, and everyone at The Hours Writers, Satellite of Love, Milk, RTB, Tonic, That's What She Said, Open Collab and Writer's Café, where many of my poems were inspired, shared and crafted.

Thanks for mentoring, attention to themes, sequence and building this manuscript go to Lucy English, Luke Palmer, Colin Brown, and Harriet Evans for helping with edits to make Fontanelle the best it can be: much appreciated. I'm thrilled with this cover, designed by Gus Cummins, and I have to thank Abby, my daughter, for lending her cradling arms.

Thanks to those who have challenged me when I've said writing is precious, when really it's often raw, visceral, painful and laboured. From the age of three I wanted to be a nurse and later a midwife. Thanks to all the 'With Women' workers, families and communities. My fingernails grip on to all those rewarding, tough and human stories. Many are celebrated here. Special thanks to midwife Sue Murphy, colleague, friend and midwife to my third.

My family are extraordinary. Pat, my beautiful mum, taught me to search inside stories, while my dad Vic taught me facts and how things fit together. They would be quietly very proud. Angie, my twin, knows my writing from a different viewpoint. Thanks to Martin, Abby and Joe for thriving on my skimmed-off mothering between midwifery and needing to write; you amaze me.

Thank you to the following publications, and their editors, teams and readers, for giving these poems their first homes and generous support of the work.

Blue of Noon (2015): 'Mundane Sunday, 1997'
Bristol After Stroke (2020): 'Wisdom in Lockdown'
Café Writers Poem of the Month (2021): 'Blue'
Finest (2021): 'Opening'
Hecate Magazine Birth Anthology (2021): 'Safe Harbour'
Hippocrates Prize (2017): 'Opening'
I Am Not a Silent Poet (2015): 'Porcelain'
Ink Sweat & Tears (2019, 2021): 'Escapades with Dad', 'Hair'
Literati Magazine (2020): 'Bubbles'
Lyrically Justified Volume 3, Urban Word Collective (2019): 'Magpies, 1880'
Our Beating Heart NHS70, erbacce-press (2018): 'Opening'
Poems from the Lockdown, Willowdown Books (2020): 'Bubbles'
These Are the Hands, Fair Acres Press (2020): 'Opening'
Tools of the Trade, Poems for New Doctors, Sottish Poetry Library (2019): 'Opening'
Voices Along the Road, Alf Dubs Children's Fund (2018): 'Porcelain', 'Child and I'